THE OPEN MEDIA PAMPHLET SERIES

THE OPEN MEDIA PAMPHLET SERIES

The Umbrella of U.S. Power

The Universal Declaration of Human Rights and the Contradictions of U.S. Policy

NOAM CHOMSKY

Series editors Greg Ruggiero and Stuart Sahulka

SEVEN STORIES PRESS / New York

Copyright © 1999 by Noam Chomsky

A Seven Stories Press First Edition,
published in association with Open Media.

Open Media Pamphlet Series editors,
Greg Ruggiero and Stuart Sahulka.

Parts of this article appeared in
Index on Censorship, July/August 1994.

Library of Congress Cataloging-in-Publication Data

Chomsky, Noam.
The umbrella of U.S. power: the universal declaration of
human rights and the contradictions of U.S. policy /
Noam Chomsky.
p.   cm. —(The Open Media Pamphlet Series: 9)
ISBN 1-888363-85-1
1. Human rights. 2. Human rights—United States. 3.
United States—Foreign relations. 4. United Nations. Gen-
eral Assembly. Universal Declaration of Human Rights. I.
Title. II. Series.
JC571.C547 1998
327.73'009'045—dc21   98-30157
                                       CIP

Book design by Cindy LaBreacht

9 8 7 6 5 4 3

Printed in Canada.

The adoption of the Universal Declaration of Human Rights (UD) on December 10, 1948, constituted a step forward in the slow progress toward protection of human rights. The overarching principle of the UD is universality. Its provisions have equal standing. There are no moral grounds for self-serving "relativism," which selects for convenience; still less for the particularly ugly form of relativism that converts the UD into a weapon to wield selectively against designated enemies.

The 50th anniversary of the UD provides a welcome occasion for reflection on such matters, and for steps to advance the principles that have been endorsed, at least rhetorically, by the nations of the world. The chasm that separates words from actions requires no comment; the annual reports of the major human rights organizations provide more than ample testimony. And there is no shortage of impressive rhetoric. One would have to search far to find a place where leadership and intellectuals do not issue ringing endorsements of the principles and bitter condemnation of those who violate them—

notably excluding themselves and their associates and clients.

I will limit attention here to a single case: the world's most powerful state, which also has the most stable and longstanding democratic institutions and unparalleled advantages in every sphere, including the economy and security concerns. Its global influence has been unmatched during the half century when the UD has been in force (in theory). It has long been as good a model as one can find of a sociopolitical order in which basic rights are upheld. And it is commonly lauded, at home and abroad, as the leader in the struggle for human rights, democracy, freedom and justice. There remains a range of disagreement over policy: at one extreme, "Wilsonian idealists" urge continued dedication to the traditional mission of upholding human rights and freedom worldwide, while "realists" counter that America may lack the means to conduct these crusades of "global meliorism" and should not neglect its own interests in the service of others. By "granting idealism a near exclusive hold on our foreign policy," we go too far, high government officials warn, with the agreement of many scholars and policy analysts.[1] Within this range lies the path to a better world.

To discover the true meaning of principles that are proclaimed, it is of course necessary to go beyond rhetorical flourishes and public pronouncements, and to investigate actual practice. Examples must be chosen carefully to give a fair picture. One useful approach is to take the examples chosen as the

NOAM CHOMSKY

"strongest case," and to see how well they withstand scrutiny. Another is to investigate the record where influence is greatest and interference least, so that we see the operative principles in their purest form. If we want to determine what the Kremlin meant by human rights and democracy, we pay little heed to *Pravda*'s denunciations of racism in the United States or state terror in its client regimes, even less to protestation of noble motives. Far more instructive is the state of affairs in the "people's democracies" of Eastern Europe. The point is elementary, and applies generally. For the United States, the western hemisphere is the obvious testing ground, particularly the Central America–Caribbean region, where Washington has faced few external challenges for almost a century. It is of some interest that the exercise is rarely undertaken, and when it is, castigated as extremist or worse.

Before examining the operative meaning of the UD, it might be useful to recall some observations of George Orwell's. In his preface to *Animal Farm*, Orwell turned his attention to societies that are relatively free from state controls, unlike the totalitarian monster he was satirizing. "The sinister fact about literary censorship in England," he wrote, "is that it is largely voluntary. Unpopular ideas can be silenced, and inconvenient facts kept dark, without any need for any official ban." He did not explore the reasons in any depth, merely noting the control of the press by "wealthy men who have every motive to be dishonest on certain important topics," reinforced by the "general tacit agreement," instilled by a good education, "that 'it wouldn't do' to mention that particular fact." As a result, "Anyone who challenges the prevailing orthodoxy finds himself silenced with surprising effectiveness."

As if to illustrate his words, the preface remained unpublished for 30 years.[2]

In the case under discussion here, the "prevailing orthodoxy" is well summarized by the distinguished Oxford-Yale historian Michael Howard: "For 200 years the United States has preserved almost unsullied the original ideals of the Enlightenment..., and, above all, the universality of these values," though it "does not enjoy the place in the world that it should have earned through its achievements, its generosity, and its goodwill since World War II."[3] The record is unsullied by the treatment of "that hapless race of native Americans, which we are exterminating with such merciless and perfidious cruelty" (John Quincy Adams[4]) or the fate of the slaves who provided cheap cotton to allow the industrial revolution to take off—not exactly through market forces; by the terrible atrocities the United States was once again conducting in its "backyard" as the praises were being delivered; or by the fate of Filipinos, Haitians, Vietnamese, and a few others who might have somewhat different perceptions.

The favored illustration of "generosity and goodwill" is the Marshall Plan. That merits examination, on the "strongest case" principle. The inquiry again quickly yields facts that "it wouldn't do to mention." For example, the fact that "as the

Marshall Plan went into full gear the amount of American dollars being pumped into France and the Netherlands was approximately equaled by the funds being siphoned from their treasuries to finance their expeditionary forces in Southeast Asia," to carry out terrible crimes.[5] And that under U.S. influence Europe was reconstructed in a particular mode, not quite that sought by the anti-fascist resistance, though fascist and Nazi collaborators were generally satisfied.

Nor would it do to mention that the generosity was largely bestowed by American taxpayers upon the corporate sector, which was duly appreciative, recognizing years later that the Marshall Plan "set the stage for large amounts of private U.S. direct investment in Europe,"[6] establishing the basis for the modern Transnational Corporations, which "prospered and expanded on overseas orders,... fueled initially by the dollars of the Marshall Plan" and protected from "negative developments" by "the umbrella of American power."[7] Furthermore, "Marshall Plan aid was also crucial in offsetting capital flight from Europe to the United States," a matter of which "American policymakers were in fact keenly aware," preferring that "wealthy Europeans" send their money to New York Banks because "cooperative capital controls had proven unacceptable to the American banking community." "The enormity of Marshall Plan aid thus did not so much reflect the resources required to rebuild Europe,... but rather the volume of funds that were needed to offset the 'mass movements of nervous flight capital'" predicted by leading economists, a flow that apparently *exceeded* the Marshall plan aid provided by American taxpayers—effectively, to "wealthy Europeans" and New York Banks.[8]

It is, again, of some interest that thoughts of that nature were "silenced with surprising effectiveness" during the 50th anniversary celebration of this unprecedented act of generosity and goodwill, the strongest case put forth by admirers of the "global meliorism" of the world's most powerful state, hence of direct relevance to the question being addressed here.

The "prevailing orthodoxy" has sometimes been subjected to explicit test, on the obvious terrain. Lars Schoultz, the leading academic specialist on human rights in Latin America, found that U.S. aid "has tended to flow disproportionately to Latin American governments which torture their citizens,... to the hemisphere's relatively egregious violators of fundamental human rights." That includes military aid, is independent of need, and runs through the Carter period.[9] More wide-ranging studies by economist Edward Herman found a similar correlation world-wide, also suggesting a plausible reason: aid is correlated with improvement in the investment climate, often achieved by murdering priests and union leaders, massacring peasants trying to organize, blowing up the independent press, and so on. The result is a secondary correlation between aid and egregious violation of human rights. It is not that U.S. leaders prefer torture; rather, it has little weight in comparison with more important values. These studies precede the Reagan years, when the questions are not worth posing.[10]

By "general tacit agreement," such matters too are "kept dark," with memories purged of "inconvenient facts."

The natural starting point for an inquiry into Washington's defense of "the universality of [Enlightenment] values" is the UD. It is accepted generally as a human rights standard. U.S. courts have, furthermore, based judicial decisions on "customary international law, as evidenced and defined by the Universal Declaration of Human Rights."[11]

The UD became the focus of great attention in June 1993 at the World Conference on Human Rights in Vienna. A lead headline in the *New York Times* read: "At Vienna Talks, U.S. Insists Rights Must be Universal." Washington warned "that it would oppose any attempt to use religious and cultural traditions to weaken the concept of universal human rights," Elaine Sciolino reported. The U.S. delegation was headed by Secretary of State Warren Christopher, "who promoted human rights as Deputy Secretary of State in the Carter Administration." A "key purpose" of his speech, "viewed as the Clinton Administration's first major policy statement on human rights," was "to defend the universality of human rights," rejecting the claims of those who plead "cultural relativism." Christopher said that "the worst violators are the world's aggressors and those who encourage the spread of arms," stressing that "the universality of human rights set[s] a single standard of acceptable behavior around the world, a standard Washington would apply to all countries." In his own words, "The United States will never join those who would undermine the Universal Declaration" and will defend its universality against those who hold "that human rights should be interpreted differently in regions with non-Western cultures," notably the "dirty dozen" who reject elements of the UD that do not suit them.[12]

Washington's decisiveness prevailed. Western countries "were relieved that their worst fears were not realized—a retreat from the basic tenets of the 1948 Universal Declaration of Human Rights..." The "Challenge of Relativity" was beaten back, and the conference declared that "The universal nature of these rights and freedoms is beyond question."[13]

A few questions remained unasked. Thus, if "the worst violators are the world's aggressors and those who encourage the spread of arms," what are we to conclude about the world's leading arms merchant, then boasting well over half the sales of arms to the third world, mostly to brutal dictatorships, policies accelerated under Christopher's tenure at the State Department with vigorous efforts to enhance the publicly-subsidized sales, opposed by 96 percent of the population but strongly supported by high tech industry?[14] Or its colleagues Britain and France, who had distinguished themselves by supplying Indonesian and Rwandan mass murderers, among others?[15]

The subsidies are not only for "merchants of death." Revelling in the new prospects for arms sales

NOAM CHOMSKY

with NATO expansion, a spokesman for the U.S. Aerospace Industries Association observes that the new markets ($10 billion for fighter jets alone, he estimates) include electronics, communications systems, etc., amounting to "real money" for advanced industry generally. The exports are promoted by the U.S. government with grants, discount loans and other devices to facilitate the transfer of public funds to private profit in the United States while diverting the "transition economies" of the former Soviet empire to increased military spending rather than the social spending that is favored by their populations (the U.S. Information Agency reports). The situation is quite the same elsewhere.[16]

And if aggressors are "the worst violators" of human rights, what of the country that stands accused before the International Court of Justice for the "unlawful use of force" in its terrorist war against Nicaragua,[17] contemptuously vetoing a Security Council resolution calling on all states to observe international law and rejecting repeated General Assembly pleas to the same effect?[18] Do these stern judgments hold of the country that opened the post-Cold War era by invading Panama, where, four years later, the client government's Human Rights Commission declared that the right to self-determination and sovereignty was still being violated by the "state of occupation by a foreign army," condemning its continuing human rights abuses?[19] I omit more dramatic examples, such as the U.S. attack against South Vietnam from 1961-62, when the Kennedy Administration moved from support for a Latin American-style terror state to outright aggression, facts that it still "wouldn't do" to admit into history.[20]

Further questions are raised by Washington's (unreported) reservations concerning the Declaration of the Vienna Conference. The United States was disturbed that the Declaration "implied that any foreign occupation is a human rights violation."[21] That principle the United States rejects, just as, alone with its Israeli client, the United States rejects the right of peoples "forcibly deprived of [self-determination, freedom and independence]..., particularly peoples under colonial and racist regimes and foreign occupation or other forms of colonial domination,... to struggle to [gain these rights] and to seek and receive support [in accordance with the Charter and other principles of international law]"—facts that also remain unreported, though they might help clarify the sense in which human rights are advocated.[22]

Also unexamined was just how Christopher had "promoted human rights under the Carter Administration." One case was in 1978, when the spokesman for the "dirty dozen" at Vienna, Indonesia, was running out of arms in its attack against East Timor, then approaching genocidal levels, so that the Carter Administration had to rush even more military supplies to its bloodthirsty friend.[23] Another arose a year later, when the Carter Administration sought desperately to keep Somoza's National Guard in power after it had slaughtered some 40,000 civilians, finally evacuating commanders in planes disguised with Red Cross markings (a war crime), to Honduras, where they were reconstituted as a terrorist force under the direction of Argentine neo-Nazis. The record elsewhere in the region was arguably even worse.[24]

Such matters too fall among the facts that "it wouldn't do to mention."

The high-minded rhetoric at and about the Vienna conference was not besmirched by inquiry into the observance of the UD by its leading defenders.[25] These matters were, however, raised in Vienna in a Public Hearing organized by NGOs. The contributions by activists, scholars, lawyers, and others from many countries reviewed "Alarming evidence of massive human rights violations in every part of the world as a result of the policies of the international financial institutions," the "Washington Consensus" among the leaders of the free world. This "neoliberal" consensus is based on what might be called "really existing free market doctrine": market discipline is of great benefit to the weak and defenseless, though the rich and powerful must shelter under the wings of the nanny state. They must also be allowed to persist in "the sustained assault on [free trade] principle" that is deplored in a scholarly review of the post-1970 ("neoliberal") period by GATT secretariat economist Patrick Low (now director of economic research for the World Trade Organization), who estimates the restrictive effects of Reaganite measures at about three times those of other leading industrial countries, as they "presided over the greatest swing toward protectionism since the 1930s," shifting the United States from "being the world's champion of multilateral free trade to one of its leading challengers," the journal of the Council on Foreign Relations commented in a review of the decade.[26]

It should be added that such analyses omit the major forms of market interference for the benefit of the rich: the transfer of public funds to advanced industry that underlies virtually every dynamic sector of the U.S. economy, often under the guise of "defense." These measures were escalated again by the Reaganites, who were second to none in extolling the glories of the free market—for the poor at home and abroad. The general practices were pioneered by the British in the 18th century and have been a dominant feature of economic history ever since, and a good part of the reason for the contemporary gap between the first and the third world (growing for many years along with the growing gap between rich and poor sectors of the population worldwide).[27]

The Public Hearing at Vienna received no mention in mainstream U.S. journals, to my knowledge, but citizens of the free world could learn about the human rights concerns of the vast majority of the world's people from its report, published in an edition of 2000 copies in Nepal.[28]

The provisions of the UD are not well-known in the United States, but some are familiar. The most famous is Article 13 (2), which states that "Everyone has the right to leave any country, including his own." This principle was invoked with much passion every year on Human Rights Day, December 10, with demonstrations and indignant condemnations of the Soviet Union for its refusal to allow Jews to leave. To be exact, the words just quoted were invoked, but not the phrase that follows: "and to return to his country." The significance of the omitted words was spelled out on December 11, 1948, the day after the UD was ratified, when the General Assembly unanimously passed U.N. Resolution 194, which affirms the right of Palestinians to return to their homes or receive compensation, if they chose not to return, reaffirmed regularly since. But there was a "general tacit agreement" that it "wouldn't do" to mention the omitted words, let alone the glaringly obvious fact that those exhorting the Soviet tyrants to observe Article 13, to much acclaim, were its most dedicated opponents.

It is only fair to add that the cynicism has finally been overcome. At the December 1993 U.N. session, the Clinton Administration changed U.S. official policy, joining Israel in opposing Resolution 194, which was reaffirmed by a vote of 127-2. As is the norm, there was no report or comment. But at least the inconsistency is behind us: the first half of Article 13 (2) has lost its relevance, and Washington now officially rejects its second half.[29]

Let us move on to Article 14, which declares that "Everyone has the right to seek and to enjoy in other countries asylum from persecution." Haitians, for example, including the 87 victims captured by Clinton's blockade and returned to their charnel house, with scant notice, as the Vienna conference opened.[30] The official reason was that they were fleeing poverty, not the rampant terror of the military junta, as they claimed. The basis for this insight was not explained.

In her report on the Vienna conference a few days earlier, Sciolino had noted that "some human rights organizations have sharply criticized the Administration for failing to fulfill Mr. Clinton's campaign promises on human rights," the "most dramatic case" being "Washington's decision to forcibly return Haitian boat people seeking political asylum." Looking at the matter differently, the events illustrate Washington's largely rhetorical commitment to "the universality of human rights," except as a weapon used selectively against others.

The United States has upheld Article 14 in this manner since Carter (and Christopher) "promoted human rights" by shipping miserable boat people back to torment under the Duvalier dictatorship, a respected ally helping to convert Haiti to an export platform for U.S. corporations seeking supercheap and brutalized labor—or to adopt the terms preferred by USAID, to convert Haiti into the "Taiwan of the Caribbean." The violations of Article 14 were ratified formally in a Reagan-Duvalier agreement. When a military coup overthrew Haiti's first democratically-elected President in September 1991, renewing the terror after a brief lapse, the Bush Administration imposed a blockade to drive back the flood of refugees to their torture chamber.[31]

Bush's "reprehensible,... illegal and irresponsible refugee policy"[32] was bitterly condemned by candidate Bill Clinton, whose first act as President was to make the illegal blockade still harsher, along with other measures to sustain the junta, to which we return.

Again, fairness requires that we recognize that Washington did briefly depart from its rejection of Article 14 in the case of Haiti. During the few months of democracy (Feb.-Sept. 1991), the Bush Administration gained a sudden and short-lived sensitivity to Article 14 as the flow of refugees declined to a trickle—in fact, reversed, as Haitians returned to their country in its moment of hope. Of the more than 24,000 Haitians intercepted by U.S. forces from 1981 through 1990, Washington allowed 28 claims for asylum as victims of political persecution, granting 11 (in comparison with 75,000 out of 75,000 Cubans). During the seven-month democratic interlude under President Aristide, with violence and repression radically reduced, 20 claims were allowed from a refugee pool 1/50th the scale. Practice returned to normal after the military coup and the renewed terror.[33]

Concerned that protests might make it difficult to maintain the blockade, the Clinton Administration pleaded with other countries to relieve the United States of the burden of accommodating the refugees. Fear of a refugee flow was the major reason offered as the "national security" interest that might justify military intervention, eliciting much controversy. The debate overlooked the obvious candidate: Tanzania, which had been able to accommodate hundreds of thousands of Rwandans, and would surely have been able to come to the rescue of the beleaguered United States by accepting a few more Black faces.

The contempt for Article 14 is by no means concealed. A front-page story in the Newspaper of Record on harsh new immigration laws casually records the fact and explains the reasons:

> Because the United States armed and financed the army whose brutality sent them into exile, few Salvadorans were able to obtain the refugee status granted to Cubans, Vietnamese, Kuwaitis and other nationalities at various times. The new law regards many of them simply as targets for deportation [though they were fleeing] a conflict that lasted from 1979 until 1992, [when] more than 70,000 people were killed in El Salvador, most of them by the American-backed army and the death squads it in turn supported, [forcing] many people here to flee to the United States.[34]

The same reasoning extended to those who fled Washington's other terrorist wars in the region.

The interpretation of Article 14 is therefore quite principled: "worthy victims" fall under Article 14, "unworthy victims" do not. The categories are determined by the agency of terror and prevailing power interests. But the facts have no bearing on Washington's role as the crusader defending the universality of the UD from the relativist challenge. The case is among the many that illustrate an omission in Orwell's analysis: the easy tolerance of inconsistency, when convenient.

Articles 13 and 14 fall under the category of Civil and Political Rights. The UD also recognizes a second category: Economic, Social, and Cultural Rights. These are largely dismissed in the West. U.N. Ambassador Jeane Kirkpatrick described these provisions of the UD as "a letter to Santa Claus... Neither nature, experience, nor probability informs these lists of 'entitlements,' which are subject to no constraints except those of the mind and appetite of their authors." They were dismissed in more temperate tones by the U.S. Representative to the U.N. Commission on Human Rights, Ambassador Morris Abram, who emphasized in 1990 that Civil and Political Rights must have "priority," contrary to the principle of universality of the UD.[35]

Abram elaborated while explaining Washington's rejection of the Report of the Global Consultations on the Right to Development, defined as "the right of individuals, groups, and peoples to participate in, contribute to, and enjoy continuous economic, social, cultural and political development, in which all human rights and fundamental freedoms can be fully realized." "Development is not a right," Abram informed the Commission. Indeed, the proposals of the Report yield conclusions that "seem preposterous," for example, that the World Bank might be obliged "to forgive a loan or to give money to build a tunnel, a railroad, or a school." Such ideas are "little more than an empty vessel into which vague hopes and inchoate expectations can be poured," Abram continued, and even a "dangerous incitement."[36]

Closely paraphrasing Abram's thesis, we may understand the fundamental error of the alleged "right to development" to be its tacit endorsement of the principle that

> Everyone has the right to a standard of living adequate for the health and well-being of himself and his family, including food, clothing, housing and medical care and necessary social services, and the right to security in the event of unemployment, sickness, disability, widowhood, old age or other lack of livelihood in circumstances beyond his control.

If there is no right to development, as defined, then this statement too is an "empty vessel" and perhaps even "dangerous incitement." Accordingly this principle too has no status: there are no such rights as those affirmed in Article 25 of the UD, just quoted.

The United States alone vetoed the Declaration on the Right to Development, thus implicitly vetoing Article 25 of the UD as well.[37]

It is unnecessary to dwell on the status of Article 25 in the world's richest country, with a poverty level twice that of any other industrial society, particularly severe among children. Almost one in four children under six fell below the poverty line by 1995 after four years of economic recovery, far more than other industrial societies,[38] though Britain is gaining ground, with "One in three British babies born in poverty," the press reports, as "child poverty has increased as much as three-fold since Margaret Thatcher was elected" and "up to 2 million British children are suffering ill-health and stunted growth because of malnutrition." Thatcherite programs reversed the trend to improved child health and led to an upswing of childhood diseases that had been controlled, while public funds are used for such purposes as illegal projects in Turkey and Malaysia to foster arms sales by state-subsidized industry.[39] In accord with "really existing free market doctrine," public spending after 17 years of Thatcherite gospel is the same as when she took over.[40]

In the United States, subjected to similar policies, 30 million people suffered from hunger by 1990, an increase of 50 percent from 1985, including 12 million children lacking sufficient food to maintain growth and development (before the 1991 recession). Forty percent of children in the world's richest city fell below the poverty line. In terms of such basic social indicators as child mortality, the United States ranks well below any other industrial country, alongside of Cuba, which has less than 5 percent the GNP per capita of the United States and has undergone many years of terrorist attack and increasingly severe economic warfare at the hands of the hemispheric superpower.[41]

Given its extraordinary advantages, the United States is in the leading ranks of relativists who reject the universality of the UD by virtue of Article 25 alone.

The same values guide the international financial institutions that the U.S. largely controls. The World Bank and the IMF "have been extraordinarily human rights averse," the chairperson of the U.N. Committee on Economic, Social and Cultural Rights, Philip Alston, observed with polite understatement in his submission to the Vienna countersession. "As we have heard so dramatically at this Public Hearing," Nouri Abdul Razzak of the Afro-Asian People's Solidarity Organization added, "the policies of the international financial institutions are contributing to the impoverishment of the world's people, the degradation of the global environment, and the violation of the most fundamental human rights," on a mind-numbing scale.

In the face of such direct violations of the principles of the UD, it is perhaps superfluous to mention the refusal to take even small steps towards upholding them. UNICEF estimates that every hour, 1000 children die from easily preventable disease, and almost twice that many women die or suffer serious disability in pregnancy or childbirth for lack of simple remedies and care. To ensure universal access to basic social services, UNICEF estimates, would require a quarter of the annual military expenditures of the "developing countries," about 10 percent of U.S. military spending.[42] As noted, the United States actively promotes military expenditures of the "developing countries"; its own remain at Cold War levels, increasing today while social spending is being severely cut. Also sharply declining in the 1990s is U.S. foreign aid, already the most miserly among the developed countries, and virtually non-existent if we exclude the rich country that is the primary recipient (Washington's Israeli client).[43]

In his "Final Report" to the U.N. Commission on Human Rights in 1996, Special Rapporteur Leandro Despouy cites the World Health Organization's characterization of extreme poverty as the world's most ruthless killer and the greatest cause of suffering on earth: "No other disaster compared to the devastation of hunger which had caused more deaths in the past two years than were killed in the two World Wars together." The right to a standard of living adequate for health and well-being is affirmed in Article 25 of the UD, he notes, and in the International Covenant on Economic, Social, and Cultural Rights, "which places emphasis more particularly on 'the fundamental right of everyone to be free from hunger'."[44] But from the highly relativist perspective of the West, these principles of human rights agreements have no status, though they are officially endorsed.

There are other differences of interpretation concerning Article 25. The U.N. Commission on Human Rights was approached by third world countries seeking means "to stem the huge flow of dangerous substances" to the poor countries, concerned that "dumping toxic products and wastes threatened the basic rights of life and good health" guaranteed by the UD. The U.N. investigator determined that the rich countries send "masses of toxic waste" to the third world and now, the former Soviet domains. "She said information she gathered shows 'serious violations of the right to life and health,'" the press reported, and "in some cases 'had led to sickness, disorders, physical or mental disability and even death.'" Her information was limited, however, because she had "little cooperation from developed countries or corporations," and none at all from the United States, which is moving to terminate her mission.[45]

Article 23 of the UD declares that "Everyone has the right to work, to free choice of employment, to just and favorable conditions of work and to protection against unemployment," along with "remuneration ensuring for himself and his family an existence worthy of human dignity, and supplemented, if necessary, by other means of social protection." We need not tarry on Washington's respect for this principle. Furthermore, "Everyone has the right to form and to join trade unions for the protection of his interests."

The latter right is technically upheld in the United States, though legal and administrative mechanisms ensure that it is increasingly observed in the breach. By the time the Reaganites had completed their work, the United States was far enough off the spectrum so that the International Labor Organization, which rarely criticizes the powerful, issued a recommendation that the United States conform to international standards, in response to an AFL-CIO complaint about strikebreaking by resort to "permanent replacement workers."[46] Apart from South Africa, no other industrial country tolerated these methods to ensure that Article 23 remains empty words; and with subsequent developments in South Africa, the United States may stand in splendid isolation in this particular respect, though it has yet to achieve British standards, such as allowing employers to use selective pay increases to induce workers to reject union and collective bargaining rights.[47]

Reviewing some of mechanisms used to render Article 23 inoperative, *Business Week* reported that from the early Reagan years, "U.S. industry has conducted one of the most successful antiunion wars ever, illegally firing thousands of workers for exercising their rights to organize." "Unlawful firings occurred in one-third of all representation elections in the late '80s, vs. 8 percent in the late '60s." Workers have no recourse, as the Reagan Administration converted the powerful state they nurtured to an expansive welfare state for the rich, defying U.S. law as well as the customary international law enshrined in the UD. Management's basic goal, the journal explains, has been to cancel the rights "guaranteed by the 1935 Wagner Act," which brought the U.S. into the mainstream of the industrial world.[48] That has been a basic goal since the New Deal provisions were enacted, and although the project of reversing the victory for democracy and working people was put on hold during the war, it was taken up again when peace arrived, with great vigor and considerable success.[49] One index of the success is provided by the record of ratification of International Labor Organization conventions guaranteeing labor rights. The U.S. has by far the worst record in the Western hemisphere and Europe, with the exception of El Salvador and Lithuania. It does not recognize even standard conventions on child labor and the right to organize.[50]

"The United States is in arrears to the International Labor Organization in the amount of $92.6 million," the Lawyers Committee for Human Rights notes. This withholding of funds "seriously jeopardizes the International Labor Organization's operations"; Washington' plans for larger cuts in International Labor Organization funding "would primarily affect the International Labor Organization's ability to deliver technical assistance in the field," thus undermining Article 23 still further, worldwide.[51]

This is only part of the huge debt to international organizations that the United States refuses to pay (in violation of treaty obligations). Unpaid back dues to the United Nations are estimated at $1.3 billion. "Our doors are kept open," Secretary General Kofi Annan writes, "only because other countries in essence provide interest-free loans to cover largely American shortfalls—not only NATO allies... but also developing countries like Pakistan and even Fiji."[52] A few weeks later, still refusing to pay, the Senate voted 90-10 that the United Nations "thank the United States for its contributions," lower its obligations, "and publicly report to all member nations how much the United States has spent supporting Security Council resolutions since Jan. 1, 1990."[53]

The illegal attack on unions in violation of Article 23 has many effects. It contributes to undermining health and safety standards in the workplace, which the government chooses not to enforce, leading to a sharp rise in industrial accidents in the Reagan years.[54] It also helps to undermine functioning democracy, as people with limited resources lose some of the few methods by which they can enter the political arena. And it accelerates the privatization of aspirations, dissolving the sense of solidarity and sympathy, and other human values that were at the heart of classical liberal thought but are inconsistent with the reigning ideology of privilege and power. More narrowly, the U.S. Labor Department estimates that weakening of unions accounts for a large part of the stagnation or decline in real wages under the Reaganites, "a welcome development of transcendent importance," as the *Wall Street Journal* described the fall in labor costs from the 1985 high to the lowest in the industrial world (Britain aside).[55]

Testifying before the Senate Banking Committee in February 1997, Federal Reserve Board Chair Alan Greenspan was highly optimistic about "sustainable economic expansion" thanks to "atypical restraint on compensation increases [which] appears to be mainly the consequence of greater worker insecurity," plainly a desideratum for a good society and yet another reason for Western relativists to reject Article 25 of the UD, with its "right to security." The February 1997 Economic Report of the President, taking pride in the Clinton Administration's achievements, refers more obliquely to "changes in labor market institutions and practices" as a factor in the "significant wage restraint" that bolsters the health of the economy.[56]

The "free trade agreements," as they are commonly mislabelled (they include significant protectionist features and are "agreements" only if we discount popular opinion), contribute to these benign changes. Some of the mechanisms are spelled out in a study commissioned by the Labor Secretariat of the North American Free Trade Agreement "on the effects of the sudden closing of the plant on the principle of freedom of association and the right of workers to organize in the three countries." The study was carried out under NAFTA rules in response to a complaint by telecommunications workers about illegal labor practices by Sprint. The complaint was upheld by the U.S. National Labor Relations Board, which ordered trivial penalties after years of delay, the standard procedure. The NAFTA study, by Cornell University Labor economist Kate Bronfenbrenner, was authorized for release by Canada and Mexico, but delayed by the Clinton Administration. It reveals a significant impact of NAFTA on strike-breaking. About half of union organizing efforts are disrupted by employer threats to transfer production abroad, for example, by placing signs reading "Mexico Transfer Job" in front of a plant where there is an organizing drive. The threats are not idle. When such organizing drives nevertheless succeed, employers close the plant in whole or in part at triple the pre-NAFTA rate (about 15 percent of the time). Plant-closing threats are almost twice as high in more mobile industries (e.g., manufacturing vs. construction).[57]

These and other practices reported in the NAFTA study are illegal, but that is a technicality, as the Reagan Administration had made clear, outweighed by the contribution to undermining the right to organize that is formally guaranteed by Article 23—or in more polite words, bringing about "changes in labor market institutions and practices" that contribute to "significant wage restraint" thanks to "greater worker insecurity," within an economic model offered with great pride to a backward world, and greatly admired among privileged sectors.

A number of other devices have been employed to nullify the pledge "never [to] join those who would undermine the Universal Declaration" (Christopher) in the case of Article 23. The further dismantling of the welfare system, sharply reduced from the '70s, drives many poor women to the labor market, where they will work at or below minimum wage and with limited benefits, with an array of government subsidies to induce employers to prefer them to low-wage workers. The likely effect is to drive down wages at the lower end, with indirect effects elsewhere. A related device is the increasing use of prison labor in the vastly expanding system of social control. Thus Boeing, which monopolizes U.S. civilian aircraft production (helped by massive state subsidy for 60 years), not only transfers production facilities to China, but also to prisons a few miles from its Seattle offices, one of many examples.[58] Prison labor offers many advantages. It is disciplined, publicly subsidized, deprived of benefits, and "flexible"—available when needed, left to government support when not.

Reliance on prison labor draws from a rich tradition. The rapid industrial development in the southeastern region a century ago was based heavily on (Black) convict labor, leased to the highest bidder. These measures reconstituted much of the basic structure of the plantation system after the abolition of slavery, but now for industrial development. The practices continued until the 1920s, until World War II in Mississippi. Southern industrialists pointed out that convict labor is "more reliable and productive than free labor" and overcomes the problem of labor turnover and instability. It also "remove[s] all danger and cost of strikes," a serious problem at the time, resolved by state violence that virtually destroyed the labor movement. Convict labor also lowers wages for "free labor," much as in the case of "welfare reform." The U.S. Bureau of Labor reported that "mine owners [in Alabama] say they could not work at a profit without the lowering effect in wages of convict-labor competition."[59]

The resurgence of these mechanisms is quite natural as the superfluous population is driven to prisons on an unprecedented scale.

NOAM CHOMSKY

The attack on Article 23 is not limited to the United States. The International Confederation of Free Trade Unions reports that "unions are being repressed across the world in more countries than ever before," while "Poverty and inequality have increased in the developing countries, which globalisation has drawn into a downward spiral of ever-lower labour standards to attract investment and meet the demands of enterprises seeking a fast profit" as governments "bow to pressure from the financial markets rather than from their own electorates," in accord with the "Washington consensus."[60] These are not the consequences of "economic laws" or what "the free market has decided, in its infinite but mysterious wisdom,"[61] as commonly alleged. Rather, they are the results of deliberate policy choices under really existing free market doctrine, undertaken during a period of "capital's clear subjugation of labor," in the words of the business press.[62]

Contempt for the socioeconomic provisions of the UD is so deeply engrained that no departure from objectivity is sensed when a front-page story lauds Britain's incoming Labor government for shifting the tax burden from "large businesses" to working people and the "middle class," steps that "set Britain further apart from countries like Germany and France that are still struggling with pugnacious unions, restrictive investment climates, and expensive welfare benefits."[63] Industrial "countries" never struggle with starving children, huge profits, or rapid increase in CEO pay (under Thatcher, double that of second-place United States)[64]; a reasonable stand, under the "general tacit agreement" that the "country" equals "large businesses," along with doctrinal conventions about the health of the economy—the latter a technical concept, only weakly correlated with the health of the population (economic, social, or even medical).

The ability to nullify unwanted human rights guaranteed by the UD should be considerably enhanced by the Multilateral Agreement on Investment (MAI) that has been under intense negotiation at the OECD since May 1995. If the plans outlined in draft texts are implemented, the world should be "locked into" treaty arrangements that provide still more powerful weapons to undermine social programs and to restrict the arena of democratic politics, leaving policy decisions more fully in the hands of private tyrannies that have ample means of market interference as well.[65] The efforts were blocked at the WTO by protests of "developing countries" that are not eager to become wholly-owned subsidiaries of great foreign enterprises. But the OECD version may fare better, to be presented to the rest of the world as a *fait accompli*, with the obvious consequences. Apart from Canada, all of this proceeded under an impressive "veil of secrecy," in the words of Sir Anthony Mason, former Chief Justice of the Australian High Court, condemning his government's decision to remove from public scrutiny the negotiations over "an agreement which could have a great impact on Australia if we ratify it."[66] The business world was intimately involved from the start, but Congress and the public were kept in the dark; wisely, in the light of public attitudes towards such arrangements, well understood by political and media leaders and "opinion makers" generally.[67]

Washington's rejection of the Economic, Social, and Cultural Rights guaranteed by the UD does receive occasional mention,[68] but the issue is generally ignored in the torrent of self-praise, and if raised, elicits mostly incomprehension.

To take some typical examples, *Times* correspondent Barbara Crossette reports: "The world held a human rights conference in Vienna in 1993 and dared to enshrine universal concepts," but progress was blocked by "panicked nations of the third world." American diplomats are "frustrated at the unwillingness of many countries to take tough public stands on human rights," even though "diplomats say it is now easier to deal objectively with human rights abusers, case by case," now that the Cold War is over and "developing nations, with support from the Soviet bloc," no longer "routinely pass resolutions condemning the United States, the West in general or targets like Israel and apartheid South Africa." Nonetheless, progress is difficult, "with a lot of people paying lip service to the whole concept of human rights in the Charter, in the Universal Declaration and all that," but no more, U.N. Ambassador Madeleine Albright (now Secretary of State) observed.[69] On Human Rights Day, *Times* editors condemned the Asian countries that reject the UD and call instead for "addressing the more basic needs for people for food and shelter, medical care and schooling"[70]—in conformity with the UD.

The reasoning is straightforward. The United States rejects these principles of the UD, so they are inoperative. By supporting these principles the Asian countries are therefore rejecting the UD.

Puzzling over the contention that "human rights extend to food and shelter," Seth Faison reviews a "perennial sticking point in United States–China diplomacy, highlighting the contrast between the American emphasis on individual freedom and the Chinese insistence that the common good transcends personal rights." China calls for a right to "food, clothing, shelter, education, the right to work, rest, and reasonable payment," and criticizes the United States for not upholding these rights—which are affirmed in the UD, and are "personal rights" that the U.S. rejects.[71]

Again, the reasoning is straightforward enough, once the guiding principles are internalized.

As an outgrowth of the popular movements of the 1960s, Congress imposed human rights conditions on military aid and trade privileges, compelling the White House to find various modes of evasion. These became farcical during the Reagan years, with regular solemn pronouncements about the "improvements" in the behavior of client murderers and torturers, eliciting much derision from human rights organizations but no policy change. The most extreme examples, hardly worth discussing, involved U.S. clients in Central America. There are less egregious cases, beginning with the top recipient of U.S. aid and running down the list. The leading human rights organizations have regularly condemned Israel's "systematic torture and ill-treatment of Palestinians under interrogation,"[72] along with apparent extrajudicial execution; legalization of torture; imprisonment without charge, for as long as nine years for some of those kidnapped in Lebanon, now declared "legal" by the High Court as a "card to play" for hostage exchange;[73] and other abuses. U.S. aid to Israel is therefore patently illegal under U.S. law, Human Rights Watch (HRW) and Amnesty International have insistently pointed out (as is aid to Egypt, Turkey, Colombia and other high-ranking recipients).[74] In its annual report on U.S. military aid and human rights, Amnesty International observes—once again—that "Throughout the world, on any given day, a man, woman or child is likely to be displaced, tortured, killed or 'disappeared,' at the hands of governments or armed political groups. More often than not, the United States shares the blame," a practice that "makes a mockery of [congressional legislation] linking the granting of U.S. security assistance to a country's human rights record."[75] Such contentions elicit no interest or response in view of the "general tacit agreement" that laws are binding only when power interests so dictate.

The United States also resorts regularly to sanctions, allegedly to punish human rights violations and for "national security" reasons. Of 116 cases of sanctions used since World War II, 80 percent were initiated by the United States alone, measures that that have often received international condemnation, particularly those against Cuba since 1961, which are by far the harshest.[76] The popular and congressional human rights programs from the early 1970s also sometimes called for sanctions against severe human rights violators; South Africa was the primary target outside of the Soviet sphere. The pressures, which were worldwide, had an impact. In 1976, the U.N. General Assembly called on the IMF to "refrain forthwith from extending credits to South Africa." The next day, at U.S.-U.K. initiative, South Africa was granted more IMF funding than all of the rest of Black Africa, in fact more than any country in the world apart from Britain and Mexico. The incoming Carter Administration attempted (in vain) to block congressional efforts to impose human rights conditions on IMF funding to South Africa (claiming that it opposed "noneconomic factors," which it introduced under fraudulent pretexts to block loans to Vietnam).[77] After much delay and evasion, sanctions were finally imposed in 1985 and (over Reagan's veto) in 1986, but the Administration "created glaring loopholes" that permitted U.S. exports to increase by 40 percent between 1985 and 1988 while U.S. imports increased 14 percent in 1988 after an initial decline. "The major economic impact was reduced investment capital and fewer foreign firms."[78]

The role of sanctions is dramatically illustrated in the case of the voice of the "dirty dozen," Indonesia. After the failure of a large-scale CIA operation to foment a rebellion in 1958, the United States turned to other methods of overthrowing the

Sukarno government. Aid was cut off, apart from military aid and training. That is standard operating procedure for instigating a military coup, which took place in 1965, with mounting U.S. assistance as the new Suharto regime slaughtered perhaps 1/2 million or more people in a few months, mostly landless peasants. There was no condemnation on the floor of Congress, and no aid to the victims from any major U.S. relief agency. On the contrary, the slaughter (which the CIA compared to those of Stalin, Hitler, and Mao) aroused undisguised euphoria in a very revealing episode, best forgotten.[79] The World Bank quickly made Indonesia its third largest borrower. The U.S. and other Western governments and corporations followed along.

There was no thought of sanctions as the new government proceeded to compile one of the worst human rights records in the world, or in the course of its murderous aggression in East Timor, which, incidentally, has somehow not entered the growing literature on "humanitarian intervention"—rightly, because there is no need for intervention to terminate the decisive diplomatic and military contribution of the United States and its allies. Congress did however ban U.S. military training after the Dili massacre in 1991. The aftermath followed the familiar pattern. Delicately selecting the anniversary of the Indonesian invasion, Clinton's State Department announced that "Congress's action did not ban Indonesia's purchase of training with its own funds," so it can proceed despite the ban, with Washington perhaps paying from some other pocket. The announcement received scant notice.[80] Under the usual "veil of secrecy," Congress expressed its "outrage," reiterating that "it was and is the intent of Congress to prohibit U.S. military training for Indonesia" (House Appropriations Committee): "we don't want employees of the U.S. Government training Indonesians," a staff member reiterated forcefully, but without effect.[81] Rather than impose sanctions, or even limit military aid, the United States, Great Britain, and other powers have sought to enrich themselves by participating in Indonesia's crimes.

Indonesian terror and aggression continue unhampered, along with harsh repression of labor in a country with wages half those of China. With the support of Senate Democrats, Clinton was able to block labor and other human rights conditions on aid to Indonesia. Announcing the suspension of review of Indonesian labor practices, Trade Representative Mickey Kantor commended Indonesia for "bringing its labor law and practice into closer conformity with international standards," a witticism that is in particularly poor taste.[82]

Also instructive is the record of sanctions against Haiti after the military coup of September 1991 that overthrew its first democratically-elected government after seven months in office. The United States had reacted to President Aristide's election with alarm, having confidently expected the victory of its own candidate, World Bank official Mark Bazin, who received 14 percent of the vote. Washington's reaction was to shift aid to anti-Aristide elements, and as noted, to honor asylum claims for the first time, restoring the normal defiance of Article 14 of the UD after the military junta let loose a reign of terror, killing thousands. The Organization of American States (OAS) declared an embargo, which the Bush Administration quickly undermined by exempting U.S. firms—"fine tuning" the sanctions, the press explained, in its "latest move" to find "more effective ways to hasten the collapse of what the Administration calls an illegal Government in Haiti."[83] U.S. trade with Haiti remained high in 1992, increasing by almost half as Clinton extended the violations of the embargo, including purchases by the U.S. government, which maintained close connections with the ruling torturers and killers; just how close we do not know, since the Clinton Administration refuses to turn over to Haiti 160,000 pages of documents seized by U.S. military forces—"to avoid embarrassing revelations" about U.S. government involvement with the terrorist regime, according to Human Rights Watch.[84] President Aristide was allowed to return after the popular organizations that had swept him to power were subjected to three years of terror, and after he pledged to adopt the extreme neoliberal program of Washington's defeated candidate.

Officials of the U.S. Justice Department revealed that the Bush and Clinton Administrations had rendered the embargo virtually meaningless by authorizing illegal shipments of oil to the military junta and its wealthy supporters, informing Texaco Oil Company that it would not be penalized for violating the Presidential directive of October 1991 banning such shipments. The information, prominently released the day before U.S. troops landed to "restore democracy" in 1994, has yet to reach the general public, and is an unlikely candidate for the historical record.[85] These were among the many devices adopted to ensure that the popular forces that brought democracy to Haiti would have little voice in any future "democracy." The Clinton Administration advertises this as a grand exercise in "restoring democracy," the prize example of the Clinton Doctrine[86]—to general applause, apart from those who see us as sacrificing too much in the cause of "global meliorism." None of this should surprise people who have failed to immunize themselves from "inconvenient facts."

The operative significance of sanctions is articulated honestly by the *Wall Street Journal*, reporting the call for economic sanctions against Nigeria. "Most Agree, Nigeria Sanctions Won't Fly," the headline reads: "Unlike in South Africa, Embargo Could Hurt West."[87] In brief, the commitment to human rights is instrumental. Where some interest is served, they are important, even grand ideals; otherwise the pragmatic criterion prevails. That too should come as no surprise. States are not moral agents; people are, and can impose moral standards on powerful institutions. If they do not, the fine words will remain weapons.

Furthermore, lethal weapons. U.S. economic warfare against Cuba for 35 years is a striking illustration. The unilateral U.S. embargo against Cuba since 1961, the longest in history, is also unique in barring food and medicine. When the collapse of the USSR removed the traditional security pretext and eliminated aid from the Soviet bloc, the United States responded by making the embargo far harsher, under new pretexts that would have made Orwell wince: The 1992 Cuban Democracy Act (CDA), initiated by liberal Democrats, and strongly backed by President Clinton while he was undermining the sanctions against the mass murderers in Haiti. A year-long investigation by the American Association of World Health found that this escalation of U.S. economic warfare had taken a "tragic human toll," causing "serious nutritional deficits" and "a devastating outbreak of neuropathy numbering in the tens of thousands." It also brought about a sharp reduction in medicines, medical supplies and medical information, leaving children to suffer "in excruciating pain" because of lack of medicines. The embargo reversed Cuba's progress in bringing water services to the population and undermined its advanced biotechnology industry, among other consequences. These effects became far worse after the imposition of the CDA, which cut back licensed sales and donations of food and medical supplies by 90 percent within a year. A "humanitarian catastrophe has been averted only because the Cuban government has maintained" a health system that "is uniformly considered the preeminent model in the Third World."[88]

These do not count as human rights violations; rather, the public version is that the goal of the sanctions is to overcome Cuba's human rights violations.

The embargo has repeatedly been condemned by the United Nations. The Inter-American Commission on Human Rights of the OAS condemned U.S. restrictions on shipments of food and medicine to Cuba as a violation of international law. Recent extensions of the embargo (the Helms-Burton Act; technically, the Cuban Liberty and Democratic Solidarity Act) were unanimously condemned by the OAS. In August 1996, its judicial body ruled unanimously that the Act violated international law.

The Clinton Administration's response is that shipments of medicine are not literally barred, only prevented by conditions so onerous and threatening that even the largest corporations are unwilling to face the prospects (huge financial penalties and imprisonment for what Washington determines to be violations of "proper distribution," banning of ships and aircraft, mobilization of media campaigns, etc.). And while food shipments are indeed barred, the Administration argues that there are "ample suppliers" elsewhere (at far higher cost), so that the direct violation of international law is not a violation. Supply of medicines to Cuba would be "detrimental to U.S. foreign policy interests," the Administration declared. When the European Union complained to the WTO that the Helms-Burton Act, with its wide-ranging punishment of third parties, violates trade agreements, the Clinton Administration rejected WTO jurisdiction, as its predecessors had done when the World Court addressed Nicaragua's complaint about U.S. international terrorism and illegal economic warfare (upheld by the Court, irrelevantly). In a reaction that surpasses cynicism, Clinton condemned Cuba for ingratitude "in return for the Cuban Democracy Act," a forthcoming gesture to improve U.S.-Cuba relations.[89]

The official stand of the Clinton Administration is that Cuba is a national security threat to the United States, so that the WTO is an improper forum: "bipartisan policy since the early 1960s [is] based on the notion that we have a hostile and unfriendly regime miles from our border, and that anything done to strengthen that regime will only encourage the regime to not only continue its hostility but, through much of its tenure, to try to destabilize large parts of Latin America."[90] That stand was criticized by historian Arthur Schlesinger, writing "as one involved in the Kennedy Administration's Cuban policy." The Clinton Administration, he maintained, had misunderstood the reasons for the sanctions. The Kennedy Administration's concern had been Cuba's "troublemaking in the hemisphere" and "the Soviet connection," but these are now behind us, so the policies are an anachronism.[91]

In secret, Schlesinger had explained the meaning of the phrase "troublemaking in the hemisphere"—in Clintonite terms, trying to "destabilize" Latin America. Reporting to incoming President Kennedy on the conclusions of a Latin American Mission in early 1961, he described the Cuban threat as "the spread of the Castro idea of taking matters into one's own hands," a serious problem, he added, when "The distribution of land and other forms of national wealth greatly favors the propertied classes" through-out Latin America, and "The poor and underprivi-leged, stimulated by the example of the Cuban revolution, are now demanding opportunities for a decent living." Schlesinger also explained the threat of the "Soviet connection": "Meanwhile, the Soviet Union hovers in the wings, flourishing large devel-opment loans and presenting itself as the model for achieving modernization in a single generation."[92]

The United States officially recognizes that "deliberate impeding of the delivery of food and medical supplies" to civilian populations constitutes "violations of international humanitarian law," and "reaffirms that those who commit or order the com-mission of such acts will be held individually responsible in respect of such acts."[93] The reference is to Bosnia-Herzegovina. The President of the United States is plainly "individually responsible" for such "violations of international humanitarian law." Or would be, were it not for the "general tacit agreements" about selective enforcement, which reign with such absolute power among Western rel-ativists that the simple facts are virtually unde-tectable.

Unlike such crimes as these, the regular Administration contortions on human rights in China are a topic of debate. It is worth noting, how-ever, that many critical issues are scarcely even raised: crucially, the horrifying conditions of work-ing people, with hundreds, mostly women, burned to death locked into factories, over 18,000 deaths from industrial accidents in 1995 according to Chi-

NOAM CHOMSKY

nese government figures, and other gross violations of international conventions.[94] China's labor practices have been condemned, but narrowly: the use of prison labor for exports to the United States. At the peak of the U.S.-China confrontation over human rights, front-page stories reported that Washington's human rights campaign had met with some success: China had "agreed to a demand to allow more visits by American customs inspectors to Chinese prison factories to make sure they are not producing goods for export to the United States," also accepting U.S. demands for "liberalization" and laws that are "critical elements of a market economy," all welcome steps towards a "virtuous circle."[95]

The conditions of "free labor" do not arise in this context. They are, however, causing other problems: "Chinese officials and analysts" say that the doubling of industrial deaths in 1992 and "abysmal working conditions," "combined with long hours, inadequate pay, and even physical beatings, are stirring unprecedented labor unrest among China's booming foreign joint ventures." These "tensions reveal the great gap between competitive foreign capitalists lured by cheap Chinese labor and workers weaned on socialist job security and the safety net of cradle-to-grave benefits." Workers do not yet understand that as they enter the free world, they are to be "beaten for producing poor quality goods, fired for dozing on the job during long work hours" and other such misdeeds, and locked into their factories to be burned to death. But apparently the West understands, so China is not called to account for violations of labor rights; only for exporting prison products to the United States.

The distinction is easy to explain. Prison factories are state-owned industry, and exports to the United States interfere with profits, unlike beating and murder of working people and other means to improve the balance sheet. The operative principles are clarified by the fact that the rules allow the United States to export prison goods. As China was submitting to U.S. discipline on export of prison-made goods to the United States, California and Oregon were exporting prison-made clothing to Asia, including specialty jeans, shirts, and a line of shorts quaintly called "Prison Blues." The prisoners earn far less than the minimum wage, and work under "slave labor" conditions, prison rights activists allege. But their production does not interfere with the rights that count (in fact, enhances them in many ways, as noted). So objection would be out of place.[96]

As the most powerful state, the United States makes its own laws, using force and conducting economic warfare at will. It also threatens sanctions against countries that do not abide by its conveniently flexible notions of "free trade." Washington has employed such threats with great effectiveness (and GATT approval) to force open Asian markets for U.S. tobacco exports and advertising, aimed primarily at the growing markets of women and children. The U.S. Agriculture Department has provided grants to tobacco firms to promote smoking overseas. Asian countries have attempted to conduct educational anti-smoking campaigns, but they are overwhelmed by the miracles of the market, reinforced by U.S. state power through the sanctions threat. Philip Morris, with an advertising and promotion budget of close to $9 billion in 1992, became China's largest advertiser. The effect of Reaganite sanction threats was to increase advertising and promotion of cigarette smoking (particularly U.S. brands) quite sharply in Japan, Taiwan, and South Korea, along with the use of these lethal substances. In South Korea, for example, the rate of growth in smoking more than tripled when markets for U.S. lethal drugs were forced open in 1988. The Bush Administration extended the threats to Thailand in 1989, at exactly the same moment that its "war on drugs" was prominently declared; the media were kind enough to overlook the coincidence, even ignoring the outraged denunciations by the very conservative Surgeon-General Everett Koop. Oxford University epidemiologist Richard Peto estimated that among Chinese children under 20 today, 50 million will die of cigarette-related diseases, an achievement that ranks high even by 20th century standards.[97]

While state power energetically promotes substance abuse in the interests of agribusiness, it adopts highly selective measures in other cases. In the context of "the war against drugs," the United States has played an active role in the vast atrocities conducted by the security forces and their paramilitary associates in Colombia, the leading human rights violator in Latin America, and the leading recipient of U.S. aid and training, increased under Clinton, consistent with traditional practice noted earlier. The war against drugs is "a myth," Amnesty International reports, agreeing with other investigators. Security forces work closely with narcotraffickers and landlords while targeting the usual victims, including community leaders, human rights and health workers, union activists, students, the political opposition, but primarily peasants, in a country where protest has been criminalized. Military support for the killers is to rise to "a record level," Human Rights Watch reported, up 50 percent over the 1996 high. Amnesty International reports that "almost every Colombian military unit that Amnesty implicated in murdering civilians two years ago was doing so with U.S.-supplied weapons," which they continue to receive, along with training.[98]

The UD calls on all states to promote the rights and freedoms proclaimed and to act "to secure their universal and effective recognition and observance" by various means, including ratification of treaties and enabling legislation. There are several such International Covenants, respected in much the manner of the UD. The Convention on the Rights of the Child, adopted by the United Nations in December 1989, had been ratified by all countries other than the United States and Somalia. After long delay, the United States did endorse the International Covenant on Civil and Political Rights (ICCPR), "the leading treaty for the protection" of the subcategory of rights that the West claims to uphold, Human Rights Watch and the American Civil Liberties Union observe in their report on continued U.S. noncompliance with its provisions. The Bush Administration ensured that the treaty would be inoperative, first, "through a series of reservations, declarations and understandings" to eliminate provisions that might expand rights, and second, by declaring the United States in full compliance with the remaining provisions. The treaty is "non self-executing" and accompanied by no enabling legislation, so it cannot be invoked in U.S. courts. Ratification was "an empty act for Americans," the HRW/ACLU report concludes.[99]

The exceptions are crucial, because the United States violates the treaty "in important respects," the report continues.[100] To cite one example, the United States entered a specific reservation to Article 7 of the ICCPR, which states that "No one shall be subjected to torture or to cruel, inhuman, or degrading treatment or punishment." The reason is that conditions in U.S. prisons violate these conditions as generally understood, just as they seriously violate the provisions of Article 10 on humane treatment of prisoners and on the right to "reformation and social rehabilitation," which the United States rejects. Another U.S. reservation concerns the death penalty, which is not only employed far more freely than the norm but also "applied in a manner that is racially discriminatory," the HRW/ACLU report concludes, as have other studies. Furthermore, "more juvenile offenders sit on death row in the United States than in any other country in the world," Human Rights Watch reports.[101] A U.N. Human Rights inquiry found the United States to be in violation of the Covenant for execution of juveniles (who committed the crimes before they were 18); the United States is joined in this practice only by Iran, Pakistan, Saudi Arabia, and Yemen. Executions are rare in the industrial democracies, declining around the world, and rising in the United States, even among juveniles, the mentally impaired, and women, the U.N. report observes.[102]

The U.S. accepted the U.N. Convention Against Torture and Other Forms of Cruel, Inhuman or Degrading Treatment or Punishment, but the Senate imposed restrictions, in part to protect a Supreme Court ruling allowing corporal punishment in schools.[103]

Human Rights Watch also regards "disproportionate" and "cruelly excessive" sentencing procedures as a violation of Article 5 of the UD, which proscribes "cruel, inhuman or degrading treatment or punishment." The specific reference is to laws that treat "possession of an ounce of cocaine or a $20 'street sale' [as] a more dangerous or serious offense than the rape of a ten-year-old, the burning of a building occupied by people, or the killing of another human being while intending to cause him serious injury" (quoting a federal judge). From the onset of Reaganite "neoliberalism," the rate of incarceration, which had been fairly stable through the postwar period, has skyrocketed, almost tripling during the Reagan years and continuing the sharp rise since, long ago leaving other industrial societies far behind. 84 percent of the increase of admissions is for nonviolent offenders, mostly drug-related (including possession). Drug offenders constituted 22 percent of admissions in federal prisons in 1980, 42 percent in 1990, 58 percent in 1992. The U.S. apparently leads the world in imprisoning its population (perhaps sharing the distinction with Russia or China, where data are uncertain). By the end of 1996, the prison population had reached a record 1.2 million, increasing 5 percent over the preceding year, with the federal prison system 25 percent over capacity and state prisons almost the same. Meanwhile crime rates continued to decline.[104]

By 1998, close to 1.7 million were in federal and state prisons, or local jails. Average sentences for murder and other violent crimes have decreased markedly, while those for drug offenses have shot up, targeting primarily African Americans and creating what two criminologists call "the new American apartheid."[105]

U.S. crime rates, while high, are not out of the range of industrial societies, apart from homicides with guns, a reflection of U.S. gun laws. Fear of crime, however, is very high and increasing, in large part a "product of a variety of factors that have little or nothing to do with crime itself," the National Criminal Justice Commission concludes (as do other studies). The factors include media practices and "the role of government and private industry in stoking citizen fear." The focus is very specific: for example, drug users in the ghetto but not criminals in executive suites, though the Justice Department estimates the cost of corporate crime as 7 to 25 times as high as street crime. Work-related deaths are six times as high as homicides, and pollution also takes a far higher toll than homicide.[106]

Expert studies have regularly concluded that "there is no direct relation between the level of crime and the number of imprisonments" (European Council Commission). Many criminologists have pointed out further that while "crime control" has limited relation to crime, it has a great deal to do with control of the "dangerous classes;" today, those cast aside by the socio-economic model designed to globalize the sharply two-tiered structural model of third world societies. As noted at once, the latest "war on drugs" targeted mostly Black males; trend lines on substance use sufficed to demonstrate that. By adopting these measures, Senator Daniel Patrick Moynihan observed, "we are choosing to have an intense crime problem concentrated among minorities." "The war's planners knew exactly what they were doing," criminologist Michael Tonry comments, spelling out the details, including the racist procedures that run through the system from arrest to sentencing, in part attributable to the close race-class correlation, but not entirely.[107]

As widely recognized, the "war on drugs" has no significant effect on use of drugs or street price, and is far less effective than educational and remedial programs. But it does not follow that it serves no purpose. It is a counterpart to the "social cleansing"—the removal or elimination of "disposable people"—conducted by the state terrorist forces in Colombia and other terror states. It also frightens the rest of the population, a standard device to induce obedience. Such policies make good sense as part of a program that has radically concentrated wealth, while for the majority of the population, living conditions and income stagnate or decline. It is, correspondingly, natural for Congress to require that sentencing guidelines and policy reject as "inappropriate" any consideration of such factors as poverty and deprivation, social ties, etc. These requirements are precisely counter to European crime policy, criminologist Nils Christie observes, but sensible on the assumption that "under the rhetoric of equality," Congress "envisions the criminal process as a vast engine of social control" (quoting former Chief Judge Bazelon).[108]

The vast scale of the expanding "crime control industry" has attracted the attention of finance and industry, who welcome it as another form of state intervention in the economy, a Keynesian stimulus that may soon approach the Pentagon system in scale, some estimate. "Businesses Cash In," the *Wall Street Journal* reports, including the construction industry, law firms, the booming private prison complex, and "the loftiest names in finance" such as Goldman Sachs, Prudential, and others, "competing to underwrite prison construction with private, tax-exempt bonds." Also standing in line is the "defense establishment,... scenting a new line of business" in high-tech surveillance and control systems of a sort that Big Brother would have admired. The industry also offers new opportunities for corporate use of prison labor, as discussed earlier.[109]

Other International Covenants submitted to Congress have also been restricted as "non self-executing," meaning that they are of largely symbolic significance. The fact that Covenants, if even ratified, are declared non-enforceable in U.S. courts has been a "major concern" of the U.N. Human Rights Committee, along with the Human Rights organizations. The Committee also expressed concern that "poverty and lack of access to education adversely affect persons belonging to these groups in their ability to enjoy rights under the [ICCPR] on the basis of equality," even for that subcategory of the UD the United States professes to uphold. And while (rightly) praising the U.S. commitment to freedom of speech, the Committee also questioned Washington's announced principle that "money is a form of speech," as the courts have upheld in recent years, with wide-ranging effects on the electoral system.[110]

The United States is a world leader in defense of freedom of speech, perhaps uniquely so since the 1960s.[111] With regard to civil-political rights, the U.S. record at home ranks high by comparative standards, though a serious evaluation would have to take into account the conditions required to enjoy those rights, and also the "accelerated erosion of basic due process and human rights protections in the United States" as "U.S. authorities at federal and state levels undermined the rights of vulnerable groups, making the year [1996] a disturbing one for human rights," with the President not only failing to "preserve rights under attack" but sometimes taking "the lead in eliminating human rights protections."[112] The social and economic provisions of the UD and other conventions are operative only insofar as popular struggle over many years has given them substance. The earlier record within the national territory is shameful, and the human rights record abroad is a scandal. The charge of "relativism" levelled against others, while fully accurate, reeks of hypocrisy.

But the realities are for the most part "kept dark, without any need for any official ban."

NOTES

1. Historian David Fromkin, *New York Times Book Review*, May 4, 1997, summarizing recent work. Thomas Friedman, *NYT*, Jan. 12, 1992.

2. Bernard Crick, *Times Literary Supplement*, Sept. 15, 1972; reprinted in Everyman's Library edition of *Animal Farm*.

3. Howard, "The Bewildered American Raj," *Harper's*, March 1985.

4. William Earl Weeks, *John Quincy Adams and American Global Empire* (Lexington: Kentucky, 1992), 193.

5. Audrey R. and George McT. Kahin, *Subversion as Foreign Policy* (New York: New Press, 1995), 30. On the British analogue, see John Saville, *The Politics of Continuity* (London: Verso, 1993), 156f.; and for the broader context, Mark Curtis, *The Ambiguities of Power: British Foreign Policy Since 1945* (London: Zed, 1995).

6. U.S. Commerce Department, 1984, cited by Howard Wachtel, *The Money Mandarins* (Armonk, NY: M.E. Sharpe, 1990), 44.

7. *Business Week*, April 7, 1975.

8. Eric Helleiner, *States and the Reemergence of Global Finance* (Ithaca, London: Cornell U. Press, 1994), 58-62. His emphasis.

9. *Comparative Politics*, Jan. 1981.

10. Chomsky and Herman, *The Political Economy of Human Rights* (Boston: South End, 1979), I, ch. 2.1.1. Herman, *Real Terror Network* (Boston: South End, 1982), 126ff.

11. Joseph Wronka, *Human Rights and Social Policy in the 21st Century* (Lanham, MD: University Press of America, 1992), citing the judgment in Filartiga v. Peña (1980). For additional cases see his "Human Rights," in R. Edwards, ed., *Encyclopedia of Social Work* (Washington: NASW, 1995), 1405-18.

12. Sciolino, *NYT*, June 15, 1993.

13. Alan Riding, *NYT*, June 26, 1993.

14. William Hartung, *And Weapons for All* (New York: Harper-Collins, 1994); Hartung, *Nation*, Jan. 30, 1995. The Congressional Research Service reported that the U.S. was responsible for 57% of

arms sales to the third world in 1992; *Financial Times*, July 23, 1993. The CRS reports further that among the 11 leading arms suppliers to the "developing countries" from 1989 to 1996, the U.S. provided over 45% of the arms flow and Britain 26%. Richard Grimmett, "Conventional Arms Transfers to Developing Nations, 1989-1996" (CRS, Washington); Jim Mann, *Los Angeles Times*, Oct. 8, 1997.

15. On British arms sales to Indonesia, which began in 1978 as the slaughter in East Timor was peaking, increasing sharply under Thatcher as atrocities continued (in Indonesia as well), see John Taylor, *Indonesia's Forgotten War: The Hidden History of East Timor* (London: Zed, 1991), 86; John Pilger, *Distant Voices* (London: Vintage, 1992), 294-323. Thatcherite policy was explained by "defence procurement minister" Alan Clark: "My responsibility is to my own people. I don't really fill my mind much with what one set of foreigners is doing to another." Ibid., 309. By 1998, Britain had become the leading supplier of arms to Indonesia, not for defense, and over the strong protests of Amnesty International, Indonesian dissidents, and Timorese victims. Arms sales are reported to make up at least a fifth of Britain's exports to Indonesia (estimated at 1 billion pounds), led by British Aerospace (Martyn Gregory, "World in Action," Granada production for ITV, June 2, 9, 1997). On Rwanda, see *Rwanda: Death Despair and Defiance* (London: African Rights, 1994).

16. Jeff Gerth and Tim Weiner, "Arms Makers See a Bonanza in Selling NATO Expansion," *NYT*, June 29, 1997.

17. International Court of Justice Year 1986, 27 June 1986, General List No. 70.

18. *NYT*, Oct. 29, 1996; *Boston Globe*, Nov. 4, 1996. *Extra!* (FAIR), Dec. 1987.

19. *Panama, Central America Report* (Guatemala), Feb. 4, 1994. The U.S. also vetoed (with Britain and France) a Security Council resolution (23 December 1989) condemning the invasion and voted against a General Assembly resolution demanding the withdrawal of the "U.S. armed invasion forces from Panama" and calling the invasion a "flagrant violation of international law and of the independence, sovereignty and territorial integrity of states" (Sean Cronin, *Irish Times*, Aug. 11, 1990). The Church estimates that over 650 victims of the intensive bombing of the poor El Chorrillo district of Panama City died in hospitals, along with unknown

numbers of others. U.S.-installed President Endara went on a hunger strike in March 1990 in protest against the failure to deliver promised economic aid. Inhabitants of El Chorrillo are suing the U.S. for damages before the Inter-American Human Rights Court. *Central America Report*, March 19, 1998.

20. For review of recently declassified and other evidence, and the interpretive reaction throughout, see Chomsky, *Rethinking Camelot* (Boston: South End, 1993) and "Hamlet without the Prince of Denmark," *Diplomatic History* 20:3, Summer 1996.

21. Assistant Secretary of State for Human Rights John Shattuck, cited by Joseph Wronka, "Toward Building Peace/Human Rights Cultures: Why is the United States so Resistant?," *American Society of International Law: Interest Group of the U.N. Decade of International Law* (Feb. 1997, no. 13).

22. Resolution of the U.N. General Assembly condemning "Terrorism Wherever and by Whomever Committed," passed 153 to 2 (U.S. and Israel opposed, Honduras alone abstaining); U.N. Press release GA/7603, Dec. 7, 1987. For discussion, see Chomsky, *Necessary Illusions* (Boston: South End, 1989), 84f.; 269ff. For more on these matters, see Chomsky, *Pirates and Emperors* (New York: Claremont, 1986; Montreal: Black Rose, 1987; Amana, 1988); Alexander George, ed., *Western State Terrorism* (London: Polity, 1991).

23. Chomsky and Herman, op. cit., I, ch. 3.4.4; Chomsky, *Towards a New Cold War* (New York: Pantheon, 1992); Taylor, op. cit.

24. Peter Kornbluh, *Nicaragua: the Price of Intervention* (Washington: Institute for Policy Studies, 1987), ch. 1; Walter LaFeber, *Inevitable Revolutions* (New York: Norton, 1983), 239. On the bloody Carter/Christopher record in El Salvador, see Chomsky, *Towards a New Cold War*, 35ff.; Herman, op. cit., 181ff.; Chomsky, *Turning the Tide* (Boston: South End, 1985), 14f., 101ff. U.S.-backed state terrorism in the region mounted sharply under Reagan, as is well known (ibid., and numerous other sources).

25. For some scattered exceptions, see note 68, below.

26. Low, *Trading Free* (New York: Twentieth Century Fund, 1993), 70ff., 271. Shafiqul Islam, *Foreign Affairs, America and the World* (Winter 1989-90).

27. For discussion, keeping to the special case of protectionism, see

Paul Bairoch, *Economics and World History* (Chicago: Univ. of Chicago Press, 1993). Among many other sources, see Frederic Clairmont's classic study, *The Rise and Fall of Economic Liberalism* (Asia Publishing House, 1960), reprinted and updated (Third World Network: Penang and Goa, 1996). On the general picture, see Chomsky, *World Orders, Old and New* (New York: Columbia U. Press, 1994, updated 1996), ch. 2. On the historic role of the state system (often military) in economic development in the U.S., see Nathan Rosenberg, *Inside the Black Box* (Cambridge: Cambridge U. Press, 1982); John Tirman, ed., *The Militarization of High Technology* (Cambridge MA: Ballinger, 1984); Merritt Roe Smith, ed., *Military Enterprise and Technological Change* (Cambridge MA; MIT Press, 1985); Richard Nelson, ed., *National Innovation Systems* (Oxford: Oxford U. Press, 1993); and numerous special studies. On the growing first/third world gap, see UNDP, *Human Development Report*, 1992, 1994. For discussion, *World Orders*, ch. 2; Eric Toussaint & Peter Drucker, eds., *IMF/World Bank/WTO, Notebooks for Study and Research* 24/5, 1995, International Institute for Research and Education, Amsterdam. On the situation internal to the U.S., see particularly the biennial publication *The State of Working America of the Economic Policy Institute*. The latest edition is Lawrence Mishel, Jared Bernstein, and John Schmitt, *The State of Working America 1996-1997* (Armonk, NY: M.E. Sharpe, 1997).

28. Women's International League for Peace and Freedom (Geneva) and International Institute for Human Rights, Environment and Development (Kathmandu), *Justice Denied!* (Kathmandu: Karnali Offset Press, 1994).

29. Jules Kagian, Middle East International, Dec. 17, 1993; Middle East Justice Network, Feb.-March 1994. On the background and status of U.N. 194, see Thomas and Sally Mallison, *The Palestine Problem in International Law* and *World Order* (New York: Longman, 1986), ch. 4.

30. Reuters, "Haiti peasant group backs UN sanctions," *Boston Globe*, June 18, 1993, page 68.

31. Carter policies, see Chomsky and Herman, op. cit., II, 54f. On subsequent years, see Americas Watch, National Coalition for Haitian Refugees, Jesuit Refugee Service/USA, *No Port in a Storm*, vol. 5.7, Sept. 1993 (N.Y., Washington). Haitian background, see inter alia, Amy Wilentz, *The Rainy Season* (New York: Simon & Schus-

ter, 1989); Chomsky, *Year 501* (Boston: South End, 1993), ch. 8; Paul Farmer, *The Uses of Haiti* (Monroe ME: Common Courage, 1994); Deidre McFadyen, Pierre LaRamèe, and North American Congress on Latin America (NACLA), eds., *Haiti: Dangerous Crossroads* (Boston: South End, 1995).

32. America's Watch et al., op. cit., 1.

33. Amy Wilentz, *New Republic*, March 9, 1992; *Year 501*, ch. 8, for further details.

34. Larry Rohter, *NYT*, April 19, 1997.

35. Wronka, "Human Rights."

36. Statement, U.N. Commission on Human Rights, on Item 8, "The Right to Development," Feb. 11, 1991.

37. Joseph Wronka, "Human Rights Postscript," *American Society of International Law: Human Rights Interest Group Newsletter*, Fall 1995.

38. Mishel et al., op. cit..

39. *Observer*, Jan. 12, 1997; *Independent*, Nov. 24, 25, 1996; *Guardian Weekly*, Jan. 5, 1997; *Observer*, Jan. 19, 1997.

40. John Plender, "An accidental revolution," *Financial Times*, Jan. 17, 1997 (42.25% of GDP, he reports, in 1978-9 and 1995-6). According to the World Bank Development Report, 1996, U.K. central government budget as percent of GNP (current) increased by close to 10% from 1980 to 1994. Comparative statistics, Gail Omvedt, *Bulletin of Concerned Asian Scholars* 29.4, Oct.-Dec. 1997.

41. Chomsky, *World Orders*, ch. 2, and *Powers and Prospects* (Boston: South End, 1996), ch. 5. UNICEF, *The State of the World's Children 1997* (Oxford: Oxford Univ. Press, 1997).

42. Ibid. UNICEF, *The Progress of Nations 1996* (New York: UNICEF House, 1996).

43. The second-ranking recipient, Egypt, is granted aid to ensure its adherence to the U.S.-Israel alliance, a core part of the system of control of the oil-producing regions, also a factor in Turkey's regular place among the top aid recipients.

44. Despouy, *The Realization of Economic, Social, and Cultural*

Rights, Commission on Human Rights, Economic and Social Council, e/CN.4/Sub.2/1996/13, 28 June 1996.

45. Elizabeth Olson, "West Hinders Inquiry on Dumping as Rights Issue," *NYT*, April 5, 1998.

46. John Hoerr, *American Prospect*, Summer 1992. See Chomsky, *Year 501*, ch. 11.

47. Keith Harper, *Guardian*, May 24, 1994; see same issue on the onerous "check off" law and other devices to undermine labor rights.

48. *BW*, "The Workplace: Why America Needs Unions, But Not The Kind It Has Now," May 23, 1994.

49. Elizabeth Fones-Wolf, *Selling Free Enterprise* (Urbana: U. of Illinois Press, 1994). On the backgrounds, see Alex Carey, *Taking the Risk out of Democracy* (Urbana: U. of Illinois Press, 1996), a collection of pioneering essays on these topics.

50. *World Labour Report 1994* (Geneva: International Labor Organization Publications, 1994).

51. *In the National Interest: 1996 Quadrennial Report on Human Rights and U.S. Foreign Policy* (New York & Washington: Lawyers Committee for Human Rights, 1996).

52. Annan, "The Unpaid Bill That's Crippling the U.N.," *NYT*, March 9, 1998.

53. Barbara Crossette, *NYT*, March 27, 1998.

54. *BW*; see note above.

55. *WSJ*, Sept. 13, 1993. On persistence of the process through the recovery of the 90s, see Mishel, Bernstein, Schmitt, op. cit..

56. Editorial, *Multinational Monitor*, March 1997.

57. Bronfenbrenner, "We'll Close," ibid., based on the study she directed: "Final Report: The Effects of Plant Closing or Threat of Plant Closing on the Right of Workers to Organize."

58. Paul Wright, "Making Slave Labor Fly," *Prison Legal News*, March 1997; *Covert Action Quarterly*, Spring 1997.

59. Alex Lichtenstein, "'Through the Rugged Gates of the Penitentiary'," in Melvyn Stokes and Rick Halpern, *Race and Class in*

the American South Since 1890 (Providence: Berg, 1994).

60. Robert Taylor, *FT*, June 13, 1997.

61. John Cassidy, "Who Killed the Middle Class?," *New Yorker*, Oct. 16, 1995.

62. John Liscio, *Barron's*, April 15, 1996.

63. Youssef Ibrahim, *NYT*, July 3, 1997.

64. Lawrence Mishel and Jared Bernstein, *The State of Working America: 1994-95* (Armonk: M.E. Sharpe, 1994).

65. On the dismantling of the Bretton Woods system (primarily at U.S./U.K. initiative from the 1970s), with its principle of regulation of capital flow in order to block attacks on social programs and stimulate trade, see Helleiner, op. cit. On modalities of contemporary market interference by state/corporate interactions, see Peter Cowhey and Jonathan Aronson, *Managing the World Economy: The Consequences of Corporate Alliances* (New York: Council on Foreign Relations Press, 1993); Winfried Ruigrok and Rob van Tulder, *The Logic of International Restructuring* (London: Routledge, 1995).

66. "Are Our Sovereign Rights at Risk?", *The Age* (Melbourne), 4 March 1998). A leaked version of the treaty was placed on the internet and distributed by public interest groups. OECD, *Multilateral Agreement on Investment: Consolidated Texts and Commentary* (OLIS 9 Jan. 1997; DAFFE/MAI/97; Confidential). See Scott Nova and Michelle Sforza-Roderick of Preamble Center for Public Policy, Washington, "M.I.A. Culpa," *Nation*, Jan. 13; Martin Khor, "Trade and Investment: Fighting over investors' rights at WTO," *Third World Economics* (Penang), Feb. 15; Laura Eggertson, "Treaty to trim Ottawa's power," *Toronto Globe and Mail*, April 3; Paula Green, "Global giants: Fears of the supranational," *Journal of Commerce*, April 23; George Monbiot, "A charter to let loose the multinationals," *Guardian* (U.K.), April 15, 1997. See Chomsky, "'Domestic Constituencies'," *Z* magazine, May 1998, for updating and further detail.

67. Ibid.

68. During the Vienna conference, see Alan Riding, "Human Rights: the West Gets Some Tough Questions," Review of the Week, *NYT*, June 20, 1993, and particularly Beth Stephens of the Center for Constitutional Rights, "Hypocrisy on Rights," *NYT*, Op-ed, June 24, 1993.

NOAM CHOMSKY

69. Crossette, "Snubbing Human Rights," *NYT*, April 28, 1996; "For the U.S., Mixed Success in U.N. Human Rights Votes," *NYT*, Dec. 18, 1995.

70. Editorial, "The New Attack on Human Rights," *NYT*, Dec. 10, 1995.

71. Faison, "China Turns The Tables, Faulting U.S. on Rights," *NYT*, March 5, 1997.

72. *Torture and Ill-Treatment: Israel's Interrogation of Palestinians from the Occupied Territories* (New York: Human Rights Watch, 1994).

73. Moshe Reinfeld, Ha'aretz, March 5, 1998. Amnesty International lists 21 Lebanese prisoners in Israeli jails, secretly brought to Israel from Lebanon from 1986 to 1994, most held without charge, the others sentenced in Israeli military courts but kept in prison after serving their sentences (Yosef Algazi, ibid.).

74. *Torture and Ill-Treatment; Human Rights & U.S. Security Assistance* (Washington: Amnesty International, May 1996).

75. Ibid.

76. Mark Sommers, "Sanctions Are Becoming 'Weapon of Choice'," *CSM*, Aug. 3, 1993. Richard Garfield, Julia Devin, and Joy Fausey, "The Health Impact of Economic Sanctions," *Bulletin of the New York Academy of Medicine* 72:2, Winter 1995.

77. Jim Morrell, Center for International Policy, *Inquiry*, April 17, 1978.

78. Gay McDougall, Richard Knight, in Robert Edgar, ed., Sanctioning Apartheid (Trenton, NJ: Africa World Press, 1990). Garfield, et al., op. cit.

79. For review, see Chomsky, *Year 501*, ch. 5. See Kahin & Kahin, op. cit., on the 1958 operations, still largely concealed in the declassified record.

80. Reuters, *NYT*, Dec. 8, 1993, a few lines on an inside page.

81. Irene Wu, *Far Eastern Economic Review*, June 30, 1994. Other forms of chicanery were revealed in 1998: Tim Weiner, "U.S. Training of Indonesian Troops Goes On Despite Ban," *NYT*, March 17; and for fuller detail, Alan Nairn, "Indonesia's Killers," *Nation*, March 30, 1998.

82. *Economist*, April 2, 1994. Counterpunch (Institute for Policy Studies), Feb. 15, March 15, 1994.

83. Barbara Crossette, *NYT*, Feb. 5, 1992.

84. Kenneth Roth, Executive Director, Human Rights Watch, Letter, *NYT*, April 12, 1997. Trade: Chomsky, *World Orders*, ch. 1.

85. John Solomon, AP, Sept. 18, 1994 (lead story), ignored by the major journals. For a detailed record, see Chomsky, "Democracy Restored," *Z* magazine, Nov. 1994.

86. National Security Adviser Anthony Lake, *NYT*, Sept. 26, 1993; Sept. 23, 1994. On the measures used to impose on the "restored democracy" the programs of Washington's defeated candidate, see Chomsky, "Democracy Restored" and Powers and Prospects, ch. 5. And for extensive detail, Lisa McGowan, *Democracy Undermined, Economic Justice Denied* (Washington: Development Gap, 1997); Laurie Richardson, *Feeding Dependency, Starving Democracy* (Boston: Grassroots International, 1997).

87. Thomas Kamm and Robert Greenberger, *WSJ*, Nov. 15, 1995.

88. *Denial of Food and Medicine: The Impact of the U.S. Embargo on Health and Nutrition in Cuba* (Washington: American Association for World Health, Executive Summary, 1997).

89. Garfield, et al., op. cit. Wayne Smith, *In These Times*, Dec. 9, 1996. Anthony Kirkpatrick, The Lancet 358:9040, Nov. 30, 1996 (Cuba Update, Winter 1997). David Marcus, "EU backs off on U.S.-Cuba trade law," *BG*, April 12, 1997. See also Joanne Cameron, "The Cuban Democracy Act of 1992: The International Implications," *Fletcher Forum*, Winter/Spring 1996; Peter Morici, "The United States, World Trade, and the Helms-Burton Act," *Current History*, Feb. 1997.

90. Morris Morley and Chris McGillion, *Washington Report on the Hemisphere* (Council on Hemispheric Affairs), June 3, 1997.

91. Letter, *NYT*, Feb. 26, 1997.

92. Foreign Relations of the United States, 1961-63, vol. XII, *American Republics*, 13f., 33.

93. Resolution proposed to the U.N. Security Council by the U.S. and other countries. Cited in *Denial of Food and Medicine*.

94. Richard Smith, "Creative Destruction: Capitalist Development and China's Environment," *New Left Review* 222, March/April 1997. The record is similar elsewhere in the region.

95. Thomas Friedman, *NYT*, Jan. 21, 23, 1993.

96. Sheila Tefft, *Christian Science Monitor*, Dec. 22, 1993. Reese Erlich, *CSM*, Feb. 9, 1994. See above, at note...

97. Philip Shenon, *NYT*, May 15; Sheila Tefft, Fazlur Rahman, *CSM*, May 25; *Multinational Monitor*, June 1994. Frank Chaloupka and Adit Laixuthai, *U.S. Trade Policy and Cigarette Smoking in Asia* (Cambridge, MA: National Bureau of Economic Research, April 1996). See Chomsky, *Deterring Democracy* (London: Verso/Vintage, 1991), chaps. 4-5, for details on 1989-90.

98. Chomsky, *World Orders*, ch. 1. Javier Giraldo, S.J., *Colombia: the Genocidal Democracy* (Monroe, ME: Common Courage, 1996). *Colombia's Killer Networks: The Military-Paramilitary Partnership and the United States* (New York: Human Rights Watch, 1996). Amnesty International, "Amnesty Action: The Colombia Papers," Winter 1997.

99. *Human Rights Violations in the United States* (New York: HRW/ACLU, Dec. 1993). Convention on Rights of the Child, see Steven Ratner, *Foreign Policy*, Spring 1998.

100. For other examples, see above at note...

101. UNICEF, *State of World's Children. Lynching in All but Name* (New York: Amnesty International, Jan. 1994). AP, *BG*, June 2, 1994. Human Rights Watch Children's Project, *United States: A World Leader in Executing Juveniles* (New York: Human Rights Watch, March 1995).

102. "U.S. executions tainted by bias, says UN report," *LAT-BG*, April 4, 1998.

103. Wronka, *Human Rights and Social Policy*, 5n.

104. Cruel and Usual (New York: Human Rights Watch, March 1997). Steven Donziger, ed., *The Real War on Crime: Report of the National Criminal Justice Commission* (New York: Harper-Collins, 1996). Reuters, *NYT*, June 23, 1997.

105. Randall Shelden and William Brown, *Criminal Justice* (Belmont CA: Wadsworth, 1997), ch. 12; their emphasis.

106. Donziger, op. cit..

107. Ibid. *Christie, Crime Control as Industry* (London: Routledge, 1993). Tonry, *Malign Neglect—Race, Crime and Punishment in America* (Oxford: Oxford U. Press, 1995). On the traditional use of the criminal justice system to control the "dangerous classes," see also Richard Bonnie and Charles Whitebread, *The Marihuana Conviction* (Charlottesville: University Press of Virginia, 1974).

108. Christie, op. cit..

109. Paulette Thomas, *WSJ*, May 12, 1994. Christie, op. cit.; Donziger, op. cit., on "the Prison-Industrial Complex"; Randall Shelden, "The Crime Control Industry and the Management of the Surplus Population," Paper at Western Society of Criminology annual meeting, Honolulu, Feb.-March 1997.

110. Wronka, "Human Rights Postscript."

111. See Harry Kalven, *A Worthy Tradition: Freedom of Speech in America* (New York: Harper & Row, 1988).

112. *Human Rights Watch World Report 1997* (New York: Human Rights Watch, 1996).

NOAM CHOMSKY

UNIVERAL DECLARATION OF
HUMAN RIGHTS

PREAMBLE

Whereas recognition of the inherent dignity and of the equal and inalienable rights of all members of the human family is the foundation of freedom, justice and peace in the world,

Whereas disregard and contempt for human rights have resulted in barbarous acts which have outraged the conscience of mankind, and the advent of a world in which human beings shall enjoy freedom of speech and belief and freedom from fear and want has been proclaimed as the highest aspiration of the common people,

Whereas it is essential, if man is not to be compelled to have recourse, as a last resort, to rebellion against tyranny and oppression, that human rights should be protected by the rule of law,

Whereas it is essential to promote the development of friendly relations between nations,

Whereas the people of the United Nations have in the Charter reaffirmed their faith in fundamental human rights, in the dignity and worth of the human person and in the equal rights of men and women and have determined to promote social progress and better standards of life in larger freedom,

Whereas Member States have pledged themselves to achieve, in cooperation with the United Nations, the promotion of universal respect for and observance of human rights and fundamental freedoms,

Whereas a common understanding of these rights and freedoms is of the greatest importance for the full realization of this pledge,

Now therefore, the General Assembly proclaims this Universal Declaration of Human Rights as a common standard of achievement for all peoples and all nations, to the end that every individual and every organ of society, keeping this Declaration constantly in mind, shall strive by teaching and education to promote respect for these rights and freedoms and by progressive measures, national anad international, to secure their universal and effective recognition and observance, both among the peoples of Member States themselves and among the peoples of territories under their jurisdiction.

ARTICLE 1

All human beings are born free and equal in dignity and rights. They are endowed with reason and conscience and should act towards one another in a spirit of brotherhood.

ARTICLE 2

Everyone is entitled to all the rights and freedoms set forth in this Declaration, without distinction of any kind, such as race, colour, sex, language, religion, political or other opinion, national or social origin, property, birth or other status.

Furthermore, no distinction shall be made on the basis of the political, jurisdictional or international status of the country or territory to which a person belongs, whether it be independent, trust, non-self-governing or under any other limitation of sovereignty.

ARTICLE 3

Everyone has the right to life, liberty and security of person.

ARTICLE 4

No one shall be held in slavery or servitude; slavery and the slave trade shall be prohibited in all their forms.

ARTICLE 5

No one shall be subjected to torture or to cruel, inhuman or degrading treatment or punishment.

ARTICLE 6

Everyone has the right to recognition everywhere as a person before the law.

ARTICLE 7

All are equal before the law and are entitled without any discrimination to equal protection of the law. All are entitled to equal protection against any discrimination in violation of this Declaration and against any incitement to such discrimination.

ARTICLE 8

Everyone has the right to an effective remedy by the competent national tribunals for acts violating the fundamental rights granted him by the constitution or by law.

ARTICLE 9

No one shall be subjected to arbitrary arrest, detention or exile.

ARTICLE 10

Everyone is entitled in full equality to a fair and public hearing by an independent and impartial tribunal, in the determination of his rights and obligations and of any criminal charge against him.

ARTICLE 11

(1) Everyone charged with a penal offence has the right to be presumed innocent until proved guilty according to law in a public trial at which he has had all the guarantees necessary for his defense.

(2) No one shall be held guilty of any penal offence on account of any act or omission which did not constitute a penal offence, under national or international law, at the time when it was committed. Nor shall a heavier penalty be imposed than the one that was applicable at the time the penal offence was committed.

ARTICLE 12

No one shall be subjected to arbitrary interference with his privacy, family, home or correspondence, nor to attacks upon his honour and reputation. Everyone has the right to the protection of the law against such interference or attacks.

ARTICLE 13

(1) Everyone has the right to freedom of movement and residence within the borders of each State.

(2) Everyone has the right to leave any country, including his own, and to return to his country.

ARTICLE 14

(1) Everyone has the right to seek and to enjoy in other countries asylum from persecution.

(2) This right may not be invoked in the case of prosecutions genuinely arising from non-political crimes or from acts contrary to the purposes and principles of the United Nations.

ARTICLE 15

(1) Everyone has the right to a nationality.

(2) No one shall be arbitrarily deprived of his nationality nor denied the right to change his nationality.

ARTICLE 16

(1) Men and women of full age, without any limi-

tation due to race, nationality or religion, have the right to marry and to found a family. They are entitled to equal rights as to marriage, during marriage and at its dissolution.

(2) Marriage shall be entered into only with the free and full consent of the intending spouses.

(3) The family is the natural and fundamental group unit of society and is entitled to protection by society and the State.

ARTICLE 17

(1) Everyone has the right to own property alone as well as in association with others.

(2) No one shall be arbitrarily deprived of his property.

ARTICLE 18

Everyone has the right to freedom of thought, conscience and religion; this right includes freedom to change his religion or belief, and freedom, either alone or in community with others and in public or private, to manifest his religion or belief in teaching, practice, worship and observance.

ARTICLE 19

Everyone has the right to freedom of opinion and expression; this right includes freedom to hold opinions without interference and to seek, receive and impart information and ideas through any media and regardless of frontiers.

NOAM CHOMSKY

ARTICLE 20

(1) Everyone has the right to freedom of peaceful assembly and association.

(2) No one may be compelled to belong to an association.

ARTICLE 21

(1) Everyone has the right to take part in the government of his country, directly or through freely chosen representatives.

(2) Everyone has the right to equal access to public service in his country.

(3) The will of the people shall be the basis of the authority of government; this will shall be expressed in periodic and genuine elections which shall be by universal and equal suffrage and shall be held by secret vote or by equivalent free voting procedures.

ARTICLE 22

Everyone, as a member of society, has the right to social security and is entitled to realization, through national effort and international co-operation and in accordance with the organization and resources of each State, of the economic, social and cultural rights indispensable for his dignity and the free development of his personality.

ARTICLE 23

(1) Everyone has the right to work, to free choice of

employment, to just and favourable conditions of work and to protection against unemployment.

(2) Everyone, without any discrimination, has the right to equal pay for equal work.

(3) Everyone who works has the right to just and favourable remuneration ensuring for himself and his family an existence worthy of human dignity, and supplemented, if necessary, by other means of social protection.

(4) Everyone has the right to form and to join trade unions for the protection of his interest.

ARTICLE 24

Everyone has the right to rest and leisure, including reasonable limitation of working hours and periodic holidays with pay.

ARTICLE 25

(1) Everyone has the right to a standard of living adequate for the health and well-being of himself and of his family, including food, clothing, housing and medical care and necessary social services, and the right to security in the event of unemployment, sickness, disability, widowhood, old age or other lack of livelihood in circumstances beyond his control.

(2) Motherhood and childhood are entitled to special care and assistance. All children, whether born in or out of wedlock, shall enjoy the same social protection.

ARTICLE 26

(1) Everyone has the right to education. Education shall be free, at least in the elementary and fundamental stages. Elementary education shall be compulsory. Technical and professional education shall be made generally available and higher education shall be equally accessible to all on the basis of merit.

(2) Education shall be directed to the full development of the human personality and to the strengthening of respect for human rights and fundamental freedoms. It shall promote understanding, tolerance and friendship among all nations, racial or religious groups, and shall further the activities of the United Nations for the maintenance of peace.

(3) Parents have a prior right to choose the kind of education that shall be given to their children.

ARTICLE 27

(1) Everyone has the right freely to participate in the cultural life of the community, to enjoy the arts and to share in scientific advancement and its benefits.

(2) Everyone has the right to the protection of the moral and material interests resulting from any scientific, literary or artistic production of which he is the author.

ARTICLE 28

Everyone is entitled to a social and international

order in which the rights and freedoms set forth in this Declaration can be fully realized.

ARTICLE 29

(1) Everyone has duties to the community in which alone the free and full development of his personality is possible.

(2) In the exercise of his rights and freedoms, everyone shall be subject only to such limitations as are determined by law solely for the purpose of securing due recognition and respect for the rights and freedoms of others and of meeting the just requirements of morality, public order and the general welfare in a democratic society.

(3) These rights and freedoms may in no case be exercised contrary to the purposes and principle of the United Nations.

ARTICLE 30

Nothing in the Declaration may be interpreted as implying for any State, group or person any right to engage in any activity or to perform any act aimed at the destruction of any of the rights and freedoms set forth herein.

G.A. res. 217A (III), U.N. Doc A/810 at 71 (1948)

Adopted at 3:00 a.m., December 10, 1948

By the General Assembly of the
United Nations (without dissent)

NOAM CHOMSKY

OTHER OPEN MEDIA PAMPHLET
SERIES TITLES AVAILABLE

CORPORATE MEDIA AND THE
THREAT TO DEMOCRACY
Robert W. McChesney
80 pages / $5.95 / ISBN: 1-888363-47-9

MEDIA CONTROL: THE SPECTACULAR
ACHIEVEMENTS OF PROPAGANDA
Noam Chomsky
64 pages / $5.95 / ISBN: 1-888363-49-5

GENE WARS: THE POLITICS
OF BIOTECHNOLOGY
Kristin Dawkins
64 pages / $4.95 / ISBN: 1-888363-48-7

GLOBALIZING CIVIL SOCIETY:
RECLAIMING OUR RIGHT TO POWER
David C. Korten
80 pages / $5.95 / ISBN: 1-888363-59-2

ZAPATISTA ENCUENTRO: DOCUMENTS FROM THE
1996 ENCOUNTER FOR HUMANITY AND AGAINST
NEOLIBERALISM
The Zapatistas
64 pages / $5.95 / ISBN: 1-888363-58-4

PROPAGANDA, INC.: SELLING AMERICA'S CULTURE TO
THE WORLD
Nancy Snow
80 pages / $5.95 / ISBN: 1-888363-74-6

A SUSTAINABLE ECONOMY FOR THE
21ST CENTURY
Juliet Schor
64 pages / $5.95 / ISBN: 1-888363-75-4

THE CASE AGAINST LAMEDUCK
IMPEACHMENT
Bruce Ackerman
80 pages / $8.00 / ISBN: 1-58322-004-6